Joyce Cary

by WILLIAM VAN O'CONNOR

Columbia University Press
NEW YORK & LONDON 1966

COLUMBIA ESSAYS ON MODERN WRITERS is a series of critical studies of English, Continental, and other writers whose works are of contemporary artistic and intellectual significance.

Editor: William York Tindall

Advisory Editors

Jacques Barzun   W. T. H. Jackson   Joseph A. Mazzeo   Justin O'Brien

Joyce Cary is Number 15 of the series.

WILLIAM VAN O'CONNOR is Professor of English and Chairman of the department at University of California, Davis, California. Among his more recent books are *The Grotesque, The New University Wits,* and *High Meadow,* a book of poems.

FOR FRAN AND GEORGE

Copyright © 1966 Columbia University Press
Library of Congress Catalog Card Number: 66-19552
Printed in the United States of America

Acknowledgment is made to Michael Joseph Ltd. for permission to quote from Joyce Cary's *Memoir of the Bobotes* (copyright 1964) and to both Michael Joseph Ltd. and Harper & Row, Inc., for permission to quote from Cary's *A House of Children* (copyright 1941, 1956), *The Moonlight* (copyright 1946, 1947), and *A Fearful Joy* (copyright 1949, 1950).

Joyce Cary

In the hands of James Joyce, Virginia Woolf, Dorothy Richardson, and D. H. Lawrence the English novel underwent a sea change. Technical innovations—the consequences of their view of man's nature—"wrecked," as Walter Allen puts it, "the structure of the novel." Yet the novel still considers its traditional subjects: man in society, moral conduct, and the complex nature of the human animal. The problem for the post-modern writer—for Graham Greene, L. P. Hartley, Elizabeth Bowen, or Joyce Cary—has been to return the novel to something like its old form without sacrificing the modernist discoveries.

If Cary's art is in the tradition of *Moll Flanders*, *Tom Jones*, *Great Expectations*, and *The Old Wives' Tale*, it is also in that established by James Joyce, Virginia Woolf, and D. H. Lawrence. The earlier authors saw their stories as complete in history, like a series of Hogarth drawings, in which an apprentice was headed for the gallows, as a criminal, or the guildhall, as lord mayor. The novelist stood aside, using his finger to gesture toward the audience, tish-tishing, or oh-ing and ah-ing, or saying, Now, my friends, we come upon something quite unexpected! Listen, watch! He was the literary midwife.

The later novelist wanted to be inside the book—and he wanted the reader to be there with him. Off we go, walking down the street with Father Conmee, and we meet Mrs.

Sheehy, wife of Mr. Sheehy, M. P. The language of Father Conmee, studied, pretentious, and "pious," gives us the man. The images and phrases running in disorder through the mind of a sentimental young woman give us Gerty McDowell. Mrs. Ramsay, looking at a brown stocking, thinks about something her husband said, or watches someone walk past the window. Faulkner has a character say, "Rat!" and we don't know whether she is addressing the man in the room with her, cussing, or giving expression to her pain; only later do we find out what "Rat!" meant. But we *were* in the room with her. Virginia Woolf wanted consciousness to be luminous, even if through a fairly opaque envelope, and luminous it has been. The moment of consciousness was held to be more important than the outline of an action, the description of a neighborhood, or the history of a family through four generations.

Cary did not want to forgo this sense of immediate life. He believed that life is in the living, here and now, in the flowing present, minute to minute. The Cary story moves quickly. We *see* as Jimson sees. We *feel* as Charley in *Charley Is My Darling* feels. Cary's imagination was empathetic, and the excitement experienced by a character electrifies the prose, illuminates a scene; it pleases, alarms, or terrifies.

As Walter Allen points out, Cary also intrudes, but not in the manner of George Eliot or Thackeray. He suggests or intimates. A delinquent character represents an aspect of all delinquency. His pedantic tutor suggests all pedantic tutors. His nonconformist politician says something general about the nonconformist mind.

Cary seems somewhere between the new and the old. The "modern" novelist tends to ask questions, not to give answers. The older novelists tended to give the answers: Society is like this; the legal system is wrong for this or that reason; and serving girls who are not circumspect can expect this! The modernist seems to say: Is this the way it is? Cary seems to say, Look, haven't you seen how certain types behave? Listen closely, and you'll hear that tone of voice that is heard all over the Empire. Or, that Mister Johnson, isn't he like impulsive, hard-driving, creative men everywhere? The generalizations are there, but they are tentative, not insisted upon.

The novelist's problem is the discovery of a satisfactory form. Cary was, in a sense, obsessed with that need. In *Art and Reality*, written for Cambridge lectures he was too ill to give, he spoke of two sorts of mind: the analytical-conceptual, and the intuitive-imaginative. Strong on theorizing, Cary would write an essay or give a radio talk at the drop of a hat. He was a great explainer. He was also an artist. Sometimes he saw a story swarm into being, coming up from some dark recesses in his mind; or he pushed his way, character by character, episode by episode, page by page, until he had a huge pile of manuscript. Sometimes, when he found the clue to form and meaning, he would cut out scenes, episodes, and even begin again, pursuing the "right sensation." He was like Lawrence in refusing to plot (anyone, he said, can plot) and in insisting on giving his demon its way. ("Trust the story," Lawrence said, "not the author.") Cary would have agreed. His problem was to keep Cary the analyst and Cary the theorizer in check, and to give Cary the intuitive-imaginative man as much freedom as he could take without fouling the reins.

In an interview published in the *Paris Review* Cary said:

The whole set-up—character—of the world as we know it. Roughly, for me, the principal fact of life is the free mind. For good and evil, man is a free creative spirit. This produces the very queer world we live in, a world of continuous creation. A perpetually new and lively world, but a dangerous one full of tragedy and injustice. A world in everlasting conflict between the new idea and the old allegiances, new arts and new inventions against the old establishment.

This explains a great deal about Cary's preoccupations as a novelist, and his search for the proper form.

Cary liked to show youth and age in conflict, one generation slipping into timelessness and watching, in a distorted fashion, the new generation coming on. To achieve this he sometimes employs a continuous-present, in something like the form Faulkner used in *Absalom! Absalom!* or in the love-story section of *The Wild Palms*. The past and present sit side by side as an early episode follows a later episode, or as they merge in a character's mind. Cary makes frequent use of flashbacks, and, often, for the sake of immediacy, employs the present tense. There is also a sense of immediacy in the way a character sees the world; it shines, like one enormous epiphany. Thus Gulley Jimson, just out of jail:

I was walking by the Thames. Half-past morning on an autumn day. Seen in a mist. Like an orange in a fried-fish shop. All bright below. Low tide, dusty water and a crooked bar of straw, chicken boxes, dirt and oil from mud to mud. Like a viper swimming in skim-milk. The old serpent, symbol of nature and love.

In a few lines Cary has caught Gulley Jimson, artist, eccentric, ardent viewer of whatever passes before him.

E. M. Forster, in an essay on Virginia Woolf, says the novel can dispense with plot. Probably he is wrong, and Cary was wrong to minimize it. Dickens is the novelist he is because he is a superb storyteller, and plot can illuminate character. Cary's characters are not so grotesque as Dickens's characters, nor does he create such a variety of them. On the other hand, although he creates them larger than life, he does not rely on caricature. There may be a limitation in Cary's characterizations in that he prefers his characters to have creative imagination. It is, he felt, one of the great treasures. This may be a limitation, but it gave Cary an affirming vision of life that thus far has been very rare in the fiction of the twentieth century. The Carys were a Devonshire family. Sir George Cary (1541–1647), who was second in command under Essex in his Irish campaign, built Castle Cary, as it was later called, about ten miles from Derry on Lough Foyle. He was, according to William R. Young, "Recorder of Derry in 1613, an office held until his death in 1647. He was M.P. for the city, 1613, and about the same time acquired considerable estate under Sir Arthur Chichester." On this estate Joyce Cary, a direct descendant, played as a child. The castle was torn down in 1964, so the present owner would not have to pay taxes on it.

Arthur Pitt Cary, Joyce's father, was an engineer, a railway consultant. His wife was the former Charlotte Joyce. Their son Joyce was born in Derry in 1888 but the small family lived in London, Arthur being the first Cary in generations to earn a living away from the family estate. There were, however, frequent visits to Ireland, and on these occasions Joyce played with his cousins, fished, hunted, listened to local workmen, rode horseback, read enormously, and dreamed.

When Joyce Cary was eight, his mother died. In England, the household of his uncle, Tristram Cary, became his family center. He still spent summers in Ireland, but the land reforms, which had begun in the 1880s, were making life difficult for the old members of the Ascendancy. Young Cary became keenly aware of incipient disaster.

Cary attended Hurstleigh preparatory school at Tunbridge Wells, then Clifton College, in Bristol. At seventeen, he went off to Paris to become a painter. (One of his friends there was J. Middleton Murry.) Cary did not take especially well to Parisian art life, and spent the next three years at the Art

School, Edinburgh. There were strong emotional tensions in Cary—one side of him was drawn toward social concerns, the other toward art. Suddenly he gave up painting, and read law in a desultory way at Trinity, Cambridge. He belonged to a crowd that did a lot of drinking and little work. During this period, he began and dropped a novel. He barely squeaked through a degree. The outside world was beckoning. The Balkan War of 1912–13 had broken out, and he went out to the Balkans to join the medical-student brother of Gertrude Ogilvie, his fiancée. The war in Montenegro, between the Christian Balkans and Islamic Turkey, was the result of the seizure of Constantinople by the Turks in 1909. The Turkish rule was so tyrannous and fiercely nationalistic that the hitherto disorganized Balkan states united. During the course of a year they more than decimated the Turks, and all but forced them from Europe.

Soon after his arrival in the Balkans, Cary was arrested as a spy. He was released when he asked to join the Red Cross, but the Red Cross officials wouldn't accept him. It was necessary, he was told, to sign up in London. Thereupon he joined the Montenegrin army and served as a cook. He saw heavy fighting and remained until the Turks surrendered at Sentari in 1913.

Somewhat later, probably before World War I, Cary wrote *Memoir of the Bobotes*, which was published only after his death. The volume, illustrated by Cary's own drawings, is the record of a young man's adventures. England, he was certain, had put behind it the stupidity of war. The Edwardian world, for all its pouter pigeon swollenness and stuffiness, was, after all, devoted to reason and comfortable well-being. Only little countries or backward big countries, he knew, relied on the gun to settle national disputes.

Cary presents a pastoral people, their soldiers and families, their valleys, towns, and mountains. He finds all of it delightfully "old world," unlike anything one could see in England. A pleasant, thoughtless innocence pervades the book. Oddly, some of it reads like Hemingway, especially the Hemingway of *The Sun Also Rises*. The dialogue is cheery, somewhat mordant, and simple:

> A tall saturnine man, very dark, with a black moustache, came in after five minutes and was presented to me as a friend of the Professor's, Lieutenant Popovic, late of the Servian army. He clicked his heels, bowed, shook hands, sat down composedly, and called for beer.
> "You are going to Cettinje," said the Professor in the tone of a man who expects to be contradicted.
> "No, Antivari. I catch the train at Virpazar."
> "To the Red Cross. You are doctor?"
> "I am not a doctor. But I am going to the Red Cross."
> "The Lieutenant desires very much to go to Antivari. He speaks the language—I am sure he could be of assistance to you—"
> "There is plenty of room in my carriage."
> The Professor looked very much delighted but at the same time embarrassed.
> "Perhaps if you would ask him—invite him. It is rather delicate. He speaks a little French."
> I asked the Lieutenant, who accepted, and went to get his bag.
> The Professor leant across the table, took me by the lapel of my coat and thanked me.

Cary's manner is that of a rather boisterous and bumptious young man who finds the natives unsophisticated if not bizarre. He enjoys looking, listening, and being involved in the entanglements and dangers of their war. The scenes are rendered vividly, and the characters caught with the objectivity of a painter good at caricature. Thematically there is little or no relation to the later work; nor is it likely the book would have seen print had Cary not gone on to become an important novelist. However, it demonstrates that Cary, even as a very young man, was a writer of terse, evocative prose. He was a sharp observer, with a twinkle in his clear blue eyes.

At the close of the Montenegrin war, Cary returned to Ireland. The Irish Land Act of 1881 had transferred land ownership to local Irish farmers. Only a few Anglo-Irish managed the shift. One of these was Sir Horace Plunkett, a man dedicated to co-operatives and technical improvement. He invited Cary's assistance but Plunkett's younger aides were not willing to accept Cary, a member of the English Ascendancy, and he was made to feel that as a nonspecialist he had nothing to offer the new cause. A few months later he applied for a post in Nigeria.

Out of sixty-four applicants, Cary was one of six to be selected. In 1913 Nigeria was still territory for slave-traders, especially Arab ones. The British Protectorate, devoted to freedom from oppression, worked hard to eliminate slave-trading, and gradually succeeded. The British were less imaginative about freedom, and in failing to provide adequate education, Cary later said, made it difficult for true freedom to find any real scope or to develop.

Assigned to the north, Cary often lived out in the bush. Gradually he learned that most administrators were satisfied if a quiet passivity obtained. Only a few of them responded to the Nigerian challenge. These began schools and built roads. Cary saw famine of a sort he had never conceived possible. Old men, quietly facing death, held infants and allowed themselves to be spoon-fed.

With the outbreak of war, the British and Germans lined up

for what, to the natives and even the Europeans, were asinine encounters in the bush and in the mountains. Cary, as a veteran soldier, was involved in all major campaigns. Sounds of the "enemy" in high grass or across a lake could turn out to be a British party out on reconnaissance. Mountains were climbed painfully—and the attackers were likely to find the defenders had gone down the other side. During one attack on a German stronghold a bullet scraped Cary's mastoid, leaving a wound from which he never recovered.

In June, 1916, Cary, home on leave, married Gertrude Ogilvie. Two months later he was back in Nigeria. Letters to his wife catch the excitement, the boredom, and the comedy—he wore a monocle, for example—of his sitting as a judge. One dark woman, to show her contempt for the court, undressed quickly and redressed very slowly. Cary also tried to write. Mornings were for work, afternoons for writing . . . and also for drinking and pondering.

During the aftermath of dengue fever he became convinced he had no real talent. His spirits picked up, however, when he read that his old friend Middleton Murry had written a pretentious novel. Still he wished he had turned solely to writing after the Montenegrin war.

Shifts in assignment gave him a variety of experiences—all of them stored away against that day when the mills of his imagination would be free to grind, and he could watch the grain flow, attempting to control the channels and bins into which it would pour in tumult. The natives and their drums might speak for offenses committed a hundred or a thousand years back in time, for atavistic aspirations and hopes. In them, Cary sought for the key to our ancient humanity.

It was 1919 before Cary, making the break, decided to

return home. There had been months of map making, bridge building, learning about juju and native beliefs about death and rebirth. All this was now over. After an editor in New York paid him £240 for several stories, he packed up and went back to England. He and his wife pooled their small incomes, £900 in all, and settled down in Oxford for what Cary knew would be a long, hard pull. The Carys moved into a large house in North Oxford, with pointed Gothic windows, and a small, thickly overgrown garden. With inflation and a growing family—there were four children—Cary was sometimes tempted to return to a post in Africa, but his wife encouraged him to continue as a writer. Without her encouragement, he said, he would probably have given up. More than a decade would pass before he sold his first novel, *Aissa Saved* (1932).

Novel followed novel, but it was not until 1941, when *Herself Surprised* was published, followed by *To Be a Pilgrim* and *The Horse's Mouth*, that Cary appeared to have won a place for himself among English novelists. It was sometimes said that he belonged in the company of Charles Dickens, Thomas Hardy, and Joseph Conrad. The kudos of success were his as these and later books won public attention.

Cary, a small, wiry man, took long walks through Oxford, continued to produce his voluminous manuscripts, and to enjoy life with his family. During World War II, he worked in Civil Defense at Oxford. In 1943 he wrote a film on Africa, *Men of Two Worlds*, and in 1946 went to India.

Gertrude Ogilvie died in 1949, and Cary, his children grown, lived on alone in the big house. There were lecture tours to America. In 1953, his youngest son, Tristram, a classical scholar, died. By then, Cary himself was suffering from muscular atrophy. In his last years he was sometimes able to move only the thumb and forefinger of his right hand. Yet he continued to write. A week before his death he could not move his fingers at all. He died on March 27, 1957.

Enid Starkie, a close friend of the Carys, remembers him as a thorough extrovert, "a man of rigid habits, supported by traditions" and a lover of "all family ceremonial." His movements were quick, and he cocked his head "like a benevolent cockatoo." She saw him as a great stoic, a man whose "gay, dynamic manner" was deliberate, but whose unconscious mood was a pervasive sadness. "As often happens with those whose view of life is sad, he had a rich fund of comedy and fun, an eye for the ridiculous and humorous situation, and a delightful irony that was the most Irish thing about him. This was sometimes of the *humour noir* variety, and, on his death bed, he joked with the irony of a Scarron."

Miss Starkie may be quite accurate in her analysis of the sources of Cary's fearful joys. He himself spoke of people being battered by life, and said that as a child he was no boxer but fortunately had had a lot of blood and was "a good bleeder." Cary as novelist is affirmative in a way that almost no other modern novelist has been. Willed or not, there is in his fiction the happy strength of characters like Gulley Jimson, Sara Monday, and Chester Nimmo; fortunately for them, they don't know when they are licked.

Joyce Cary looked upon himself as a political writer whose subject was freedom. Nineteenth-century liberals defined liberty as freedom from restraint. Cary defined it as freedom to create. Thus a government that keeps a child in school until he is sixteen or eighteen is giving him an opportunity to create, because a fuller development of his talents can mean a life of greater vitality, enjoyment, and usefulness. Again, assuming freedom is the goal, bothersome activity—the din of hammers or the sound of jet engines or the smoke from factories—may mean progress. Freedom grows out of conflict.

In *Power in Men* (1939), Cary attacked nationalism for its false propaganda, for veiling, hiding, or misrepresenting facts. He attacked all systems—from Plato's Republic to Hitler's Germany—that deny the individual his right to create, and govern by coercion. The individual has the need for insights and access to new knowledge that transcends the righteous insistence of the dictator that his will, his "facts," his dogmas are the truth.

Cary believed that attempted checks upon liberty, upon "the advance of democratic peoples" will fail. The checks produce "violence, war, or revolution." Man, though often misguided, misled, or deluded, seeks freedom. "To fight liberty," he said, "is to oppose the power of nature itself." All over the globe, man was driven by a need to know the truth. Monolithic governments would be overthrown.

Cary's world of liberty is not, however, utopian; it is often tragic. Man is free to choose, and to choose wrongly. Good men are destroyed. Civilizations crumble. We live in change. "This turmoil," he said, "is what we pay for being free creative souls." Yet one should not, must not, give up. The great power in men is the force that strives for freedom, for fuller opportunities. Man is creative. When churches, schools, or governments impose a fixed, a static order, this need for freedom, this power rises, and eventually the restraints are broken.

During the 1930s and 1940s, Cary was a member of the Liberal Party. He was asked to write on African colonialism for the Liberal Book Club. He had decided against using Africa as the setting for further novels, and therefore felt that a nonfiction study would help him to write fiction untrammeled by being too analytical or abstract, at the expense of the intuitive and imaginative.

The Case for African Freedom appeared in 1941 and was enlarged in 1944. In both editions he developed the thesis stated in *Power in Men*, that freedom is man's destiny, and constitutes his "field of power." He argues that the African requires what the Caucasian or Oriental requires, the extension of freedom. The individual African needs education, the power to earn a just return for his services or his enterprise, and the right to be engaged in a modern economy, based on a democratic political system.

In January, 1943, Cary went to East Africa to work on the film for the Ministry of Information *Men of Two Worlds*. (During part of the journey he worked on *The Horse's Mouth*.) Cary chose the slopes of Kilimanjaro as his setting and the local people as a part of his cast. Unfortunately, the only print of these sequences was lost en route to America, and the final version was largely done in a studio.

During the 1943 trip Cary visited Nigeria, Uganda, and Tanganyika. Daily he became more convinced that democracy had to be widely and quickly extended in Africa. He argued this in the revision of *The Case for African Freedom*, and in *Britain and West Africa*, written for Longmans in 1946.

As a young man in Nigeria, Cary had accepted the paternalism that wanted Africans to be free from European civilization and the vulgarities of a cash economy. But history had changed all that—the tribal units were breaking up, and the African himself was asking to be a part of the twentieth century. The African wanted a more abundant life, and wanted the instruments to bring it about: scientific farming and a sense of African history and his own religious heritage. The African wanted his own schools and universities. As Cary put it in his preface to *The African Witch*, like any other men the Africans were determined "to create some glory and dignity for themselves and those they love."

Among Cary's manuscripts is one called *Daventry*. Clearly it is indebted to some of Conrad's African tales, and perhaps to *Lord Jim*. In 1916, Cary wrote to his wife that he was to go out on a patrol into Muri Province, where a young Assistant District Officer, Maltby, had been killed, his head left in a juju house. Against advice, the young man, a romantic innocent, had gone into a pagan village to collect some unpaid taxes. Conrad might have said that Daventry's trek was a journey into his own soul and consciousness: he did not know the territory; he did not know himself. Cary was cynical about Daventry's public-school values. One virtue of Cary's later vision is in his setting the joy of creative freedom against the world's cruelties, irrationalities, and fortuitous injustices. But there is no range or resilience in *Daventry*.

Daventry is relatively short. The next unpublished novel, *Cock Jarvis*, is very long. It is another example of a novel that goes on and on because the author is not sure about what he is doing. In 1956, Cary said the manuscript was in "massive ruins" and he no longer expected to get a clue to its meaning. His problem was in confusing a Maugham-like love story—two men and a woman in darkest Africa—and an ill-understood political story.

Cock Jarvis as a character continued to engage Cary. He used him in Bewsher in *An American Visitor* and in *Castle Corner*, but he never found the "intuition, the approach, and the form" to catch him. Finally he put *Cock Jarvis* away in the attic.

M. M. Mahood, in an excellent study of Cary's African novels, says, "A novelist's imagination needs to be larger than his philosophy." With *Aissa Saved*, Cary's imagination overtook his love of analysis and his habit of walking a thesis like a tightrope.

Aissa Saved, like Melville's *Pierre*, Greene's *Power and the Glory*, and certain other novels, does not quite come off—but it is memorable. There are far too many characters clinging to the edges of an essentially simple story line. Aissa, a young convert, leads her fellow Christians in a holy war against the human-sacrificing juju pagans across the river. Ali, the young Moslem follower of the District Officer Bradgate, is murdered by the Christians. Aissa, trying to prove the superiority of Christianity, sacrifices her baby in a rain-making ceremony. More than seventy characters "support" this story action. Aissa is eaten alive by ants.

The theme, as Cary develops it, is in a sense antireligious. Cary appears to despise the piety of "I am not worthy, Lord!" and the self-abnegation and self-sacrifice that make suffering an escape. Mr. Carr, a missionary, retreats into virtuous defeat, welcoming it. Bradgate is contemptuous of Mrs. Carr's decision to have her baby in Africa, knowing it is likely to die from malaria. The Moslems also enjoy defeat and suffering.

Aissa Saved presents the British philosophy of Let's-get-on-with-the-job, or the conviction, shared by Conrad, that certain simple virtues, such as duty and self-respect, keep society going and help redress wrongs. But during the years of writing *Aissa Saved*, Cary discovered that each of us lives in his own "special fog" and has needs "true" for him.

Is the title *Aissa Saved* wholly ironic? Miss Mahood does not think so. Aissa destroyed her child to prove the foolishness of the rain-making ritual. Then, wanting to see her child in heaven—riding the Holy Goat—she willingly gives her life. Aissa expresses maternal love, certainly a necessary virtue. And Hilda Carr gives her life to strengthen Aissa's belief. Certainly Cary is not saying that religious persecution is necessary or that all self-sacrifice is noble—but merely that these two women, caught up in a belief not of their own creation, are "noble."

One irony is that the missionaries bring death, both to the pagans and to the converts. Yet we make choices. Later, Cary would say that Christianity should come to Africa, not because it is perfect but because it is a vehicle for European civilization, for schools and hospitals, for bringing Africa into the twentieth century. Some might object to this as hypocrisy, but Cary's God belongs to no sect.

An American Visitor (1933), concerned with white rule in Africa, has less explosive vitality than *Aissa Saved*. Perhaps there are two keys to this: the novel is too argumentative; and one of the principal characters, the American Marie Hasluck, is almost incredible. There are District Officer Bewsher; Gore, his assistant; a missionary couple; Frank Cotter, in Nigeria to make a fortune in tin; and Marie Hasluck, trained as an anthropologist, doing a series of articles for American newspapers. Each has his notions about the Birri, the tribe among whom they work.

Bewsher loves the Birri, and hopes to keep them away from the paths of civilization. Marie Hasluck, remarkably simple-minded for an anthropologist, believes in their romantic primitiveness. In fact, her conduct causes the action to sound like a melodramatic dialogue between followers of Rousseau and followers of Cecil Rhodes. She falls in love with Bewsher, marries him, fears the increasingly hostile Birri, suffers malaria, and is converted to Christianity. Under its influence, she hides Bewsher's pistol, and he is killed.

Miss Mahood quotes a letter Cary wrote to his publisher:

In this story of a modern American girl with the political and religious prejudices of her time and country, we see a passionate love affair and a religious creed growing on the same root as a political idea; each the necessary and complementary expression of the same personality, which is itself characteristic of a national atmosphere. The story of Marie Hasluck is therefore a commentary and sidelight upon American civilization and its preoccupations; but as she moves in a British dependency, falls in love with a British official and is involved therefore in local politics, the action raises also urgent and important questions of imperial policy and development.

It seems likely that Cary failed to bring Marie Hasluck to life not merely because he did not know much of anything about Americans but because his own ideas about the Birri seem, in their way, to be almost as romantic as those of Marie Hasluck.

The African Witch, as Miss Mahood says, is Cary's attempt, in creating "a whole state alive with dissension and treachery," to match *Nostromo*. Each novel is a large, splendid canvas, suggesting life and possibilities beyond what is explicitly said, and each lives in the memory long after the last page has been read.

Cary's scene is Rimi, the capital, its palace, muddy streets, crowded huts, and juju houses. The Emir is old and senile. Two factions struggle to name his successor. One claimant is Aladai, a student at Oxford, whose sister Elizabeth is a leading juju priestess. The other is Sale, favored by the British Resident Burwash. Aladai hurries home. He has the support of his sister and Coker, a missionary, a sort of Watch Tower bloodletting ranter. Once Sale is nominated, the old Emir is poisoned. Soon the palace is deserted. This is the scene in which the death of the old man is described:

At the first light of dawn the Emir had returned to the marketplace, on the west side.

He knocked at a door near the middle of that side. At the same time another door, further down, was opened, and a girl came out with a calabash. The door shut quickly behind her. She was dressed like a bride, but she appeared in the last stages of terror. She walked a few steps, then she fell on her knees.

The Emir came up to her, took the calabash, and said, "Thank you, my child. I was hungry."

He asked her what had happened to all the people. Had they run away? She answered, "No, King." But he didn't attend to her. He took the calabash, collapsed on his hams, and ate without ceremony. The girl crept away, and knocked on a door. But the door did not open. She went on creeping away, crouching almost to the ground, till she came to the main road and disappeared into it.

The Emir suddenly dropped the calabash and gave a scream; jumped to his feet and ran about twenty yards, screaming; then he fell down, rolled over on his back, kicked up his little legs, and lay dead in that position, like a beetle.

There are many similar scenes, equally eerie and grotesque.

Two worlds are in conflict: the British, pragmatic, polo-playing, and romantic about pagan culture; and the African, scheming, realistic, and believing in witchcraft. Irrationality lurks not only beneath the rituals of the witch-hunting Africans but beneath the cheerio-old-boy manners of the public-school types.

Aladai says the African does not know how to "fight sickness and pain and grief." He needs to be taught "to be free." Yet when Burwash refuses to support him, Aladai wants a war of blood, and it is his priestess sister who tells him that self-immolation is utter foolishness.

Memorable as many scenes and characters are, *The African Witch* probably is overly schematized. Whether consciously or not, it is clear that Cary finally wants to divide humanity into two groups—the African, given to self-immolation and blood-letting; and the European, dedicated to the life of reason. With *Mr. Johnson*, his final African novel, Cary creates a character whose skin is black but whose drives, ambitions, asininities, and wild imagination are neither black nor white but merely human.

Cary has been criticized for writing a patronizing book about an ignorant and naive black man, Mister Johnson. But the novel, *Mister Johnson*, is no such thing. Cary does Johnson the honor of treating him as a wildly creative man, the sort of human being that delighted Cary.

Mister Johnson is Cary at his simplest, with a minimum of political and sociological theorizing. Mister Johnson, a joyful creator—of happiness and his own destruction—is a pure Cary type, indifferent to consequences, driven, and imaginative.

Mister Johnson apparently took a long time to evolve in Cary's imagination. There are notes about him as a character as far back as the late 1920s. Two actual people, clerks Cary had known and respected, merged into one character, and finally into a fictional archetype. Mister Johnson is joyful, dedicated, given to weakness of various kinds—and lost between two worlds, white and black. In failure he is magnificent:

"Oh Gawd! O Jesus! I done finish—I finish now—Mister Johnson done finish. . . . Why you so big bloody dam' fool, you Johnson?"

Even in disaster, as a murderer, he finds joy. He *lives*, whereas those around him—the police, his friend Rudbeck, his wife, his creditors—merely exist or respond in stereotyped and conventional ways. Mister Johnson is his own legend, and he creates it moment by moment. "He gives a hop in his chair, coming down hard on his bottom, laughs, puts his head on one side and licks his lips as if tasting a good thing." He loves an audience, pursues glory, is naive, and perhaps excessively good-natured, but, in contrast, those about him seem overly careful, bored, selfish, and unloving. Mister Johnson's follies are his triumphs.

Mister Johnson loves everything that is spare, strange, unusual, unique. The Europeans, such as Rudbeck's wife, see abstractly. She calls Mister Johnson a Wog, because he is an African and is therefore like other Africans. She too creates, but in a negative, neurotic way. Rudbeck is hard-driving but is creative only when inspired by Johnson. Together the two men build a road. The day-by-day adjustments, improvisations, and victories over laziness, boredom, and bureaucracy originate with Mister Johnson.

The road itself is symbolic, an act of creation. It opens up the bush for trade, for social intercourse, for new experiences, for civilization. It will also bring evils. But, Cary says, liberty invites choice, and is therefore to be preferred over stagnation.

Johnson, the force behind Rudbeck, used unorthodox methods, including bribes, to effect the completion of the road. Rudbeck, a man of small imagination, dismisses Johnson, who takes to crime, killing Gollop, the storekeeper. Yet Rudbeck knows, and occasionally admits to himself, that Mister Johnson is a "good man," and that he, not Rudbeck, is responsible for the road. When forced to sit as Johnson's judge he feels guilty, dejected, and shrunken. In the end, Rudbeck is able to re-establish his old relationship with Johnson, by executing him.

But Rudbeck, growing ever more free in his inspiration which seems already his own idea, answers obstinately, "I couldn't let anyone else do it, could I?"

Mister Johnson is what he is, a vitality that recreates its environment and refuses to be a *thing*. He is victimized but declines the role of being a victim. Mister Johnson belongs with Charley Brown, Gulley Jimson, and Sara Monday. Life is in the living, in response to happiness and terror, in joyful sadness, and in creating the moment for the moment's sake. This, as Miss Mahood says, is the inspiration Cary found in Africa:

> Above all this African art of living consisted in an amazingly fruitful response to other people, creative of acts and gestures which were still fresh in Cary's mind twenty years later, a source of inspiration as well as a benediction.

Charley Is My Darling (1940) is Cary's first novel with an entirely English setting. Charles Brown is a fourteen-year-old lower-class Londoner sent out to Devonshire to avoid the bombings. The west of England is very foreign to him, but Charley, a creative delinquent, sets out to dominate it. His head is shaved because he has had lice, but despite his appearance, he leads a pack of children (some of them natives of the area and some from London), through a series of attacks on the adult world of bourgeois proprieties. The children, working at night, are like a raiding party, with a young Sir Francis Drake at their head. Their aim is pillage.

Charley is naive, childlike, moody, imaginative, resourceful, and a charmer. At fifteen he falls in love with Liz, a deaf girl, a young version of Sara Monday or Nina Nimmo. Her reason for being is serving and helping Charley. She submits to his sexual advances, petting, loving, and mothering him whenever possible. Her pregnancy is discovered after Charley and his clan have been hauled into court for various crimes, including wrecking a house.

Cary says all children are delinquents. This may be true, but Charley's shocked disbelief when he is severely reprimanded for getting Liz pregnant is likely to surprise most readers. It is true that neither of his parents has made any real effort to make him respect the rules of society, but even a fifteen-year-old "delinquent" would certainly be knowledgeable about the possible consequences of getting a young girl pregnant.

Enid Starkie finds the novel "sentimental and false, based on textbook psychology." Although this is rather strong criticism, there is some basis for it. Charley's adolescent imagination, his nocturnal prowlings, his destructiveness, his shyness, and his childlike collapses into sleep are all quite credible, but his failure to foresee consequences seems to contradict the shrewdness that makes him an effective leader. The child-woman Liz is also a little incredible, too much a product of Cary's conviction about the "eternal feminine."

Despite its weaknesses, *Charley Is My Darling* is a pleasure to read. Written in the present tense, it races along, with characters and actions tumbling together helter-skelter—until the day of retribution arrives. Charley and Liz are memorable characters. The mixture of formidableness, authority, and sympathy on the part of the police, the passivity of Charley's mother, his father's air of being a disciplinarian, and the bemused inability of the adults generally to understand or control the various children—all this is presented credibly. There are genuinely poignant scenes, especially those in which Charley and Liz peer backward at their childhood and forward into the murky world of their futures. Cary has the courage and the insight to look squarely at the world of adolescence, and at the delinquency of all of us, young, middle-aged, and old.

A House of Children (1941) was obviously a favorite of Cary's and some critics find it superior to *Charley Is My Darling*. There is a wonderful evocation of childhood, especially that of the hypertensive, hard-driving, wildly imaginative child Joyce Cary was. He had an artist's eye. Before it, the earth turns like a great globe of yellow, green, and blue water, racing against stone walls, into caves, or turning boats upside down. There are near-drownings, and there are wonderfully comic scenes of man, child, or animal hanging on precariously at the edge of the world. For example, a description of Roffey, an Irish Viking, and his dinghy:

> What was splintered water-worn timber had entered into his idea of himself as a rough mastery and commanded both his surly aloofness and his sudden uncalled-for fist.
> At last, with the fearful tilting of the boat, thrust over till the sheet cut the waves, we slipped off the gunwale, and fell down into the opposite side, hollow beneath us.
> Black bilge water, floating dirt and oil and fish scales, had spurted through the gratings, and into this we slid. We were all startled. Harry, who detested slimy or dirty things, looked surprised and turned red; Kathy cried out in a disgusted voice: "But I'm sitting in the water."
> This made us all laugh so much that we remained sitting in the water, leaning against the sides of the boat and stretching bare, filthy legs up the gratings, as if in an armchair. Even Kathy began to laugh and put her arms round us on both sides as if to say: "I'm with you."
> The cows had fallen together in a heap and uttered loud moos, the boxes had tumbled; a young emigrant girl sitting above us with her new, long button boots dangling in mid-air, was speaking. But no one could hear her in the wind which was roaring and shrieking at once, the tremendous swish of the water like a thousand whips, the mooing of the cows and the clatter of the boxes. She was perhaps talking to herself, or for herself alone.

The years move along; there are love affairs, marriages, children off to school, middle-aged aunts whose characters undergo very obvious changes, nude bathing. One girl develops a sudden dedication to the piano; one or another in the group is pointlessly persecuted. Someone makes a serious discovery of drama and poetry. All undergo an insweeping, across the lough, of maturity, and fitful needs for change;

one decides on a foolish elopement, another on becoming the outstanding student in a class.

Cary was often asked, he said, whether *A House of Children* was autobiographical. He said it was, although the names are changed and he divided himself into two characters. Yet finally it is not a novel. *A House of Children* provides, nonetheless, a look into Cary's consciousness, and his understanding of children. More especially, it provides an image of the turbulent, callous, exciting world—whether Northern Ireland, Nigeria, Devon, or Oxfordshire—that dominated Cary's consciousness and imagination.

As Andrew Wright points out, *A House of Children* and *Herself Surprised*, both published in 1941, are connected. Pinto, the tutor, is a preparation for Gulley Jimson. Both are anarchists, at war with society, although Pinto (whose real name is Freeman) is a talker and not an artist. In *The Horse's Mouth*, Cary used the same incident of borrowing a friend's flat and then pawning everything in it. The two men are creators of joy and of damnation. They exhibit the Cary vision of the human being caught by seemingly inexorable forces that give way, to whatever extent they do, only before his anger, his willfulness, and his refusal to be passive or resigned.

Cary's style necessarily carries within it much of the fury, excitement, exuberance, and vitality of his characteristic subject matter. In the early books, Cary intrudes with his often didactic comments, like a George Eliot or an Anthony Trollope, but with his first trilogy—*Herself Surprised, To Be a Pilgrim,* and *The Horse's Mouth*—subject becomes, or at least controls, style. Each narrator explains his own actions and those of others, and does it in his own idiom, reflecting his own privately created world. The pervasive irony of the trilogy does not arise from one set of lies being revealed by a true version, but by our inability to be at all certain about our capacity to know the truth. Lawrence Durrell uses a somewhat similar device in *The Alexandria Quartet*, but he seems more concerned with setting a complementary bizarre event against an earlier version of what happened, and therefore a general air of factitiousness pervades the four novels. Cary's characterizations are poignantly "true," whether in Sara Monday's, Gulley Jimson's, or Tom Wilcher's versions of the "truth."

Each character is caught and held in his own sensibility. In this way, each is the "modern hero," free and yet not free. Loving, generous, feminine, guileful, and yet unwitting, Sara Monday is, as many readers have observed, a modern Moll Flanders. Each supplies rationalizations as fast as they are necessary but, as Wright observes, Sara is not the sort of cheat that Moll is. Moll loves money. Sara loves men and domesticity. She is milk and cream and the occupier of a warm bed, into which Gulley or Wilcher, or any lonely stray would be welcomed. She cannot understand the harsh rules of courts or the connivings of families over money, although connivings of her own sort are so natural to her that she never questions the reasons behind them. Sara is a human criticism of *officialdom*. She is Nature, female flesh and female season, and she is Love. The reader could come to feel that for Sara Monday moral distinctions of a certain kind are really irrelevant: her virtues do not merely transcend her vices, they transform them. As Cary said, "The everlasting enterprise which was her undoing was also her salvation."

To Be a Pilgrim, Wilcher's story, supplements Sara's story. Wilcher is very English, mindful of place (Tolbrook, the family estate) and family tradition. He is dedicated and protestant, chilled and inhibited, but he is also a sensitive and, in intent, a loving man. His family-feeling causes him to allow the arrest of Sara, who steals to help Gulley Jimson, but he knows that Sara has "saved my soul alive," and perhaps he should be seen as a weak man powerless to act. He hopes that upon her release from prison they will be reunited.

Wilcher is really Sara's student. He has been deeply religious, but unlike his sister Lucy he could not undertake the desperate dedication of a "Benjamite faith"; unlike his brother Edward, he could not accept nihilism, or, on the other hand, the simple-minded commitment of his soldier brother, Bill. As he nears death, Wilcher comes to realize that change must come, "and this change, so bitter to me, is a necessary ransom for what I keep." Life is motion, is change, and cannot, except at great cost to the emotions, be abstracted. Sara was born knowing this. Wilcher, who has crept into Sara's bed and watched her in her kitchen, learns it too late.

Gulley Jimson's volume, *The Horse's Mouth*, is a portrait of a certain type of artist, the man who creates, offering up grandmothers, other people's walls, or money, wholly indifferent to the needs of any but himself. Cary seems to have liked or at least been highly amused by scoundrels like Gulley Jimson. It was enough apparently that they followed the "law" of their being. Their Law, as Auden said in one of his poems, is Me.

Cary has a vision of the *poète maudit*, the man who sees more clearly than society, who has the word from the horse's mouth. He is the modern figure of the artist, Byron, Shelley, Poe, Baudelaire, Joyce, or Pound. Very explicitly Gulley Jimson is a Blakean hero. He creates . . .

"I saw all the deaf, blind, ugly, cross-eyed, limp-legged, bulge-headed, bald and crooked girls in the world, sitting on little white mountains and weeping tears like sleet. There was a great clock ticking, and every time it ticked the tears all fell together with a noise like broken glass tinkling in a plate. And the ground trembled like a sleeping dog in front of the parlour fire when the bells toll for a funeral."

Gulley belongs to the romantic tradition—and this may suggest why he may seem just a little unreal. Interesting though he is, he does not exist in the same way that Sara or Wilcher exists. He is a period version of the artist, whereas Sara, female sexuality and evasiveness, and Wilcher, caught in a dream of his past, are eternal types.

Perhaps in Gulley Jimson we can see Cary's vision and its limitations. The world tumbles, turns, is filled with injustice, and yet has its joys, in male and female flesh, in shared sympathies, and even in a distanced anguish. Each man searches for possibilities, to create, to be free. But the artist, like Gulley, sees more, and is therefore freer. Cary's characters experience tragic gaiety and agonized joys. Gulley lives thus and preaches this doctrine. What one misses in him, or in Mister Johnson or Charley Brown, is restraint, a reaching toward peace and serenity. Life must be met and accepted, with all its injustice, harshness, and anguish; and no modern fictional characters, with the exception of some of Faulkner's, show this better than Cary's. Yet there may be something rather forced about such characters, as though Cary really looked upon passivity, or even serenity, as evasions of responsibility. Cary turns away from Keats's figures on the urn.

Proust had recorded the change and decline of the *haut monde* and the high *bourgeoisie*, imperturbable and largely incapable of responding to forces they half saw but preferred not to recognize. Ford Madox Ford performed a somewhat similar analysis and dramatization, not so much of social decay as of institutional fumbling and British philistinism, especially in the upper reaches of society. Both writers described societies they saw to be on the decline. With *Castle Corner* (1938), Cary wrote a novel, intending a trilogy, about the decline of empire. The whole would, he believed, cover history from 1880 to 1935, sweeping down through the decades. But the performance, despite piles of manuscript, failed the intention.

Cary was given to trying to force more material into the sequence of a story than character, theme, pace, or plot could comfortably accommodate. The wild, vital life, or the innocuous lassitude, of a given character struggles—and sometimes doesn't struggle—to join the forward motion of a story. In *Castle Corner* inchoate scenes—in this case in Northern Ireland, England, and Africa—touch one another. Beginnings come to little, and things appear not to mean much.

Cary himself was, of course, an Anglo-Irishman, more committed to England than to Ireland. The reader is not more than a few pages into *Castle Corner* before he realizes how profoundly the English caste system influenced and controlled the Anglo-Irishman's view of his role. The novel opens with pious John Corner viewing Deity, Empire, and Northern Ireland:

> For old John, at eighty-three, brought up in the eighteen twenties, God the Father was the ruling conception of life. God was Father of creation, the King was father of his people, and he, John, was father of his tenants, both English and Irish, especially the Irish at Castle Corner. He found them helpless and foolish children.

Possibly a clue to the breakdown in the perspective of *Castle Corner* is this unquestioned superiority. Felix, old John's son, is an "intellectual," impressive in figure yet wholly ineffectual in controlling his affairs. He goes out to Africa "on business," and soon, in the process of losing most of the family's fortune, finds his main business to be in "satisfying" the frequent needs of his black servant-wife. On a visit to England, he says, envisioning "two brown breasts," that he must return to his affairs in Africa. Cleeve, his son, much like him, has an affair with Bridget, an Irish Catholic servant. When she becomes pregnant, Cleeve takes off for Oxford, and English social life. John Chass, old John's son, who inherits the castle, is pleasant, bumbling, and ineffectual. There is Benskin, a South African new millionaire, who is like the peasant entrepreneur in *The Cherry Orchard*, a figure in contrast to the ineffectual Corners. But, again, he does not "lead" the action.

The Boer war, land reforms, the threat of revolution, comprising the intended historical panorama, are *there* and yet not there. In *Vanity Fair* the panoramic flow of Waterloo "works" —the characters swim, drown, or drive or fail to drive their horses or carriages through it. The historical panorama of *Castle Corner* does not work. One feels caught up in the asinities of Oxford types, received class opinion, the Empire "out theah"—and somehow Cary's imagination can never distance it. The weight of it sinks whatever vision his free imagination might have made of all of it.

The Moonlight (1946), a second chronicle, followed *Castle Corner* by a good many years. Some of Cary's best fiction was published in the interval. *The Moonlight*, Cary said, had two sources. It began as an infuriated reply to Tolstoy's *Kreutzer Sonata*. Cary saw Tolstoy as obsessed, one, by his need for female flesh, and, two, by a perverted desire "to abolish sexual attraction." In Tolstoy's story a jealous old man tells how he murdered his wife and "blames the education of women for the marriage market." Cary planned a reply in which sexual attraction, and women's need and right to fulfill themselves as sweethearts, lovers, and mothers is justified.

After five or six chapters, the first version was put aside. Much later, Cary was attracted by the story of a girl left in charge of a family, who sacrifices her own happiness for them. He also wanted to show the "different sexual ideas" of two or three generations. Hence, the weaving together of a Victorian strand with one about the 1920s. We see the "woman who serves," "the woman who rebels," and "the woman who is taught to conform."

The Moonlight attempts a unified story line and theme, as well as an explicit thesis, but ends up as something less than a satisfactory novel. Cary believed the role of woman in the Victorian world conformed to the needs of her nature. Women in the 1920s he saw as wanting to be chic; they became boyish, and, frequently, in their desire to compete with men, all but unsexed. In the preface to the Carfax edition, the "modern business woman" is seen as combining the Victorian "female" with the 1920s woman, whose desire is to discover herself in the arts, or science, or business. This latter generation does not "exist" in the novel. And so one is not certain what Cary's intention is. Obviously it has to do with the "eternal feminine," but exactly what this meant to him is not clear.

All of the women, even the snippy intellectuals, seem to dissolve when a clever young engineer of their passions decides to seduce them. There is something altogether too easy about the way they succumb. Here, for example, is Amanda, listening to and watching a scene that is Lawrence pastiche:

Down below, the paddock had disappeared in a deep blue-green darkness. Nothing could be seen of the mowers. But the noise of their scythes had an extraordinary loudness and regularity.

A seduction scene—of Amanda, the young scholar historian,

by Harry, a man of whom Lawrence would have said "Pan is not fallen"—is strangely unreal and forced, if only because the props are so familiar.

"No, no, it's nothing to mind."

"No, of course not," reassuring Harry or herself, she did not know which, but she thought dreamily, "No, it's nothing to mind, not this part of it. What is serious is what comes after." Bessie's face seemed to float before her, followed by a vision of the Wicken family. "A woman's life, a real woman with husband and children—that is really serious, terribly, terribly serious. You can't get over it, never."

She saw Harry's cap against the sky, he had not troubled to take it off. She reflected, "Isn't he even going to kiss me first—but no, he isn't very religious. Or, perhaps, it's because—he is so religious, yes, medieval—they used to dance and juggle in church. Oh God, I am so tired, I could scream, scream."

The Moonlight seems a dress rehearsal for *A Fearful Joy*. Ella, seduced by a non-joyous Bonser, has an illegitimate child, Amanda. Ella and Amanda, lesser Tabithas, serve their nature —"You must admit," she [Amanda] interrupted, "that women are rather specially constructed—for a purpose." The falseness of that sentence suggests the forced nature of *The Moonlight*. One wonders what might have resulted if Joyce Cary had followed his original impulse and written a novel about female sexuality and not worried about relating it to the Victorians, or to the postwar young women so determined to relate their sexuality to a new and "modern" world.

One reviewer of *A Fearful Joy* (1949) called it "a very good novel. I think it may be a great novel. . . ." Others have said, or implied, that in characterizing one decade after another for sixty years, and in presenting a "miscellany" of historical events, the novel lacks a central focus. If it does lack such a focus, so do *Moll Flanders* and *Tom Jones*. They are episodic, held together by Moll and Tom, and their lusty engagements in jail, at table, or in bed.

In Tabitha and Bonser, Cary has created two memorable characters. E. M. Forster says the merely capable novelist can create characters that live on the page and begin to die after the reader closes the book. The true novelist creates characters that live in the memory. Tabitha and Bonser live in the memory. Tabitha Baskett, a dull and not especially pretty girl, has an enormous capacity for accepting change, deflecting harmful events, and, when she wishes, ignoring figures that move larger than life across a decade or fashions that dominate an era. Dick Bonser, an opportunist, a rake, a charmer, and, for Tabitha, an irresistible force, bringing anguish and joy, accepts the world as his oyster. We watch the two, from youth to old age, and admire their comic, joyous, grotesque responses to sex, success, failure, the "delinquency" of the newest generation, to money, to health, to illness, and to death. As an American poet said of himself, they "dance with William Blake, for love, for love's sake"—and for life's sake too.

Certain of Cary's critics refer to his "inconclusiveness," his "irresolution" and the "indefiniteness" of his conclusions. There is a basis for using each or all of these terms. E. M. Forster has spoken of the dialectic in novels, at least in his own novels, and when we speak of theme we usually mean the resolving of a dialectic. T. S. Eliot decried Lawrence's characters because they did not represent moral integers—but Lawrence was trying for something else. So, too, is Cary.

A not inappropriate term to be used if one wishes to be negative about Cary is naturalism. For all of his *joie de vivre*, furious vitality, and Blakean joy, he is a kind of naturalist. His characters do not wrestle with the angel all night, carefully pick or choose, or scrupulously weigh alternatives. Life is force. Lust, parenthood, money, success, fighting, warmth, hope, despair—these and fifty more forces are the currents, the eddies, the streams in which lives flow.

Nineteenth-century naturalists, outside of their fiction, tended to preach a meliorist doctrine, were socialists, and believers in science. In their fiction, they present forces—atavisms, diseases, the country, the city, the beast in man—and a background glowering darkly, with reddish flames threatening destruction. Man lived at the edge of despair. Cary's naturalism is of a different sort. His Bonsers and Tabithas live their lives fully, joyously. Defeats, despair, humiliations, and anger are leavened by joy. Wars come and go. So too the Liberals and the Conservatives. Art movements flourish and fade. Newspapers wage campaigns against child labor, against the Hun, for Irish home rule, or for understanding of the black masses. The lives of Bonser and Tabitha are affected, or not affected. They go on living, suffering and enjoying.

For example, the concluding paragraphs of *A Fearful Joy:*

But right in her path there stands a small square girl, a child so square that Tabitha's eyes are instantly caught by the spectacle. She is very fair, and her hair, clipped round, makes square edges upon her projecting scarlet ears. Her body is square, her arms are square, her plump hands are square, her thick, absurdly short legs are two oblongs, her freckled eyebrowless face, with its insignificant nose and two large dirty tears hung mysteriously upon its square brick-red cheeks, is completely square, and she has in the middle of it a square hole, astonishingly large and square, for a mouth. And now from this hole issues a tremendous ear-splitting yell of misery and protest against the whole world, the very universe; a yell so powerful that it causes the child itself to reel sideways, in one block.

Tabitha is seized with laughter. She can't help laughing, an irresistible passion of laughter shakes her whole body, and at once a tearing pain shoots through to her heart. She thinks, "Stop—stop—it's killing me—I'm dying," and sinks breathless upon a seat.

She is protesting with all her might against this laughter, this life which has taken hold of her, but still she is full of laughter. Her very agony is amused at itself. She presses her hand to her heart as if to grasp that frightful pain in her fingers and squeeze it back, crush it out of existence. She is terrified that it will kill her, and never has she wished so ardently to live. Her whole being prays to be reprieved this once—for a month, a week, till that letter comes from Nancy.

And the prayer that is torn from her is not to the Father or the Son or the Spirit. It is the primitive cry of the living soul to the master of life, the creator, the eternal. "Oh, God," her blue lips murmur, "not quite now."

Gradually the pain becomes less, the terror falls away before the longing, the prayer. She perceives that she is not going to die that afternoon. And as, cautiously straightening her back, she looks again at the sky, the trees, the noisy quarreling children, at a world remade, she gives a long deep sigh of gratitude, of happiness.

The moral ambiguity of Nina Nimmo is a part of the complexity of the political trilogy that includes *Prisoner of Grace* (1952), *Except the Lord* (1953), and *Not Honour More* (1955). She is at once one of the most anomalous and yet credible characters Cary created. No one, least of all she, could explain the "logic" of her conduct. Sara Monday is female affection and adaptability; Nina is both and more. She is the irreducibly human who loves as she hates, and has a sense of involvement in comically grotesque actions from which she neither wills to be nor can be free.

Nina writes "her book" because of revelations to be made in the press about Chester, her former husband. This device seems unpromising. But once the story begins, staccato-like, illogical, cutting off actions not really delineated much less explained, the reader becomes a prisoner of Nina's need to protect Jim, her irascible, stupid, honor-ridden lover, and to protect Chester, crafty, driven, sincere, and with a touch of genius. She justifies her *ménage à trois*.

Nina, pregnant by Jim Latter, marries Chester for the sake

of her unborn child. Never really liking him, she fights, placates, and admires him. For thirty years she lives with him, until she finds a "solid" reason for divorcing him and marrying Jim Latter. But, remaining loyal to Chester, she submits to his libidinous attacks on her, in chairs, on couches, all within the possible notice of secretaries and typists. The seventy-year-old Chester, writing his memoirs, is at one minute like a male monkey suddenly aroused by a bent-over female monkey, but a few moments later he is a sedate "great man," a statesman reviewing his career for posterity, and writing it in piously rhetorical sentences. Nina is bound by their mutual outrages and successes, by the strings of thirty years.

Some critics have found Nina a self-indulgent liar, and it is true that as a liar she has few peers. But she is something more than this. She knows life beneath the proprieties, and she knows that politics, of which she is a symbol, never, or rarely, black or white, is filled with delusion, cant, false rhetoric, compromise, pride, sincerity, and profound commitment to ideals.

This political trilogy may, in the long run, come to appear Cary's major achievement, more moving and more convincing than the earlier trilogy. If this proves to be the case, the character Nina will be one of the keys to its success. She pursues her version of justice in a madly unjust world, the possible in a world of impossibilities, and even attempts to mediate between irreconcilable views, such as those of Chester and those of Jim Latter.

Except the Lord is Chester Nimmo's account of his own life, especially the early formative years in Devonshire. Chester's mother, a gentle, devoted woman, died from tuberculosis, and so did sister Georgina, at twenty-two, following upon the nursing of her father in the family's damp cottage. The father, a failed farmer, becomes a failed preacher. As a child, Chester, his brother Richard, and Georgina twice await the dawn and the Second Coming. Chester's firm evangelical faith receives a "mortal wound." But the family's devotion to each other, and the intensity of their love have marked Chester for life. He sees those years as the explanation of what he is, or at least what he *thinks* he is.

A profound imprint was also made on him when he and Georgina saw *Maria Marten*, a melodrama in which a rich and brutal man rapes and kills a young, poverty-stricken girl. Chester was awe-struck by the language of the play, and the monstrous injustice—but also by the villain, for whom he felt a "fascinated admiration."

Walter Allen says, and undoubedly he is right, that Cary represents the English Protestant Nonconformist tradition. In an interview Cary once said he believed in a personal God who actively involves Himself in human affairs. If He did not exist, there was no accounting for the universe or man's dual needs for beauty and justification. Cary was assured of God's presence. The title *To Be a Pilgrim* is from Bunyan:

> Who would true valour see
> Let him come hither;
> One here will constant be,
> Come wind, come weather.
> There's no discouragement
> Shall make him once relent
> His first avowed intent
> To be a pilgrim.

The Nonconformist tradition explains Wilcher and Jimson and Nimmo—and it explains Cary's preoccupation with William Blake. Allen says: "The Protestant or Nonconformist tradition, though its manifestations change from generation to generation, has been one of the most potent and formative in English life, in politics no less than in religion."

The individual, responsible only to God, suspicious of priest, ritual, and orthodoxy, goes his lonely way. To the nonbeliever he appears more than a little mad, an egotist, and often a hypocrite. He passes beyond the Slough of Despond, he climbs hills to catch sight of God's dawn, and refuses to sell his soul to Mammon.

In another century, Cary might have been a preacher. Moral tags seem to be just beneath the surface of his views—"Judge not, that ye be not judged," or "The ways of God are exceeding strange"—but he restrains himself from uttering them in the older way. Yet the half-suppressed fury, the iconoclasm, the search for one's *own* God are there, in Gulley Jimson's drive to create, come hell or high water, in Wilcher's scruples at the same time he is facing up to his own dishonesty and pettifogging ways, and in the ambiguous moralizing and self-seeking of Nimmo.

In his last novel, Cary turned to Nonconformity again, very explicitly, as though making one final effort to understand his own subject.

"When in his soliloquies at the front of the stage, his eyes, roving over the audience, seemed to meet mine, they sent forth an indescribable thrill—it seemed that something flashed from the very center of evil into my deepest soul."

In that combination—a man marked by poverty, deep religious belief, and profound family affections—we have one clue to Nimmo, the dedicated politician. In his awareness of the mesmeric effect of work we have another. And lastly, there is his admission that he felt an "indescribable thrill" at being confronted by evil.

Nimmo is not a simple character. As a young union man

he is shocked by duplicity, yet he can accept his own dishonesty, and even the political usefulness of violence. He can be very proper, and he can be obscene. He can be courageous and he can fake a heart attack for a temporary advantage. He is indifferent to Nina, and woefully dependent upon her. He can cajole, blackmail, lie, and see his own role as dedicated statesman in an aureole of religious light. Cary seems to be saying that Nimmo is *all* of these things, and no single characteristic or action cancels out the others. Nina, out of a higher social class, does not understand him because she does not *feel* his childhood. And Jim Latter, for whom everything is black or white, can see him only as a devious scoundrel, a flannel-mouthed liar, and a political opportunist.

In his narrative *Not Honour More*, we get a further look at Nimmo, from the point of view of a soldier who happens also to be more than a little mad.

Jim Latter is a bemused fanatic, convinced of his own honor and rectitude. He had allowed Nimmo to marry Nina and to be the father of his own child, and he later seduces her again. When he learns that Chester, then over seventy, and Nina are having sexual relations his sense of honor is outraged, and he kills her. Yet, as he insists, it is not merely sexual jealousy that impels him, like an avenging angel; it is that even after her retreat from Chester, she cannot resist giving him her public support, conniving with him for what she considers good ends. Jim cannot bear this. Nina and he, he insisted, were up against something bigger than either of them, "the truth."

Latter's narrative, in laconic, soldierlike prose, is dictated to Policewoman Martin as he awaits execution. The style is effective because, one, the reader has already had two earlier versions of the events, and, two, Latter is so obviously lacking in either complexity of mind or plain mother wit.

The three volumes represent Cary's view of the political world, its dependence on human relationships, the driving force of sex, and of religion. Latter is a persistent type, a believer in simple answers, and so is Nimmo, a "wrangler," as Cary called him. Nina too is a persistent type, picking her way, making choices in a world full of dilemmas and joyous possibilities. In the three novels, Cary once again presents the rush, the anguish, and the splendor of human life.

Cary wrote *The Captive and the Free* during the last three years of his life. More than once he despaired of finishing it. Five months before his death, he said, "The novel's in the bag," and for the next two months he worked at it. Perhaps it was finished in the sense that it had "emotional continuity." But it is not a "finished" novel. Certain statements are repeated unnecessarily. Hardly any of the characters are, in James's sense, "rendered." Preedy, the faith-healer protagonist is "dark skinned." Occasionally one "hears" his rhetoric, or his conceited delight, or his flashes of honesty. But he is not visible to the mind's eye. Syson, the Anglican minister, his antagonist, is like Jim Latter in *Not Honour More*, a Cary type, dedicated, obsessed, and, like Preedy, more than a little mad. Alice Rodker, seduced at fourteen by Preedy and his occasional mistress thereafter, has a face that registers terror quickly. But Hooper, a vindictive little man, full of quirks, who readily rationalizes his lusts and ambitions at the expense of others, is most readily "seen." The newspaper world itself, a sinister *deus ex machina* throughout the action, seems conventionally fake. Even the name, *The Argus*, sounds unconvincing. However, Hooper is not a central character. Nor is Joanna Rideout, his mistress and later his wife. But she is fairly well realized, as the plain, rather simple girl, who does not like Hooper and doesn't want to marry him, but who goes off weekends with him, gets pregnant despite his warnings not to, and who gratefully succumbs to marriage when the prospect of a year on the Continent pretending to be a widow seems too much. Hooper and Joanna are good minor figures.

The lustful, mendacious, self-deluding minister is hardly new to fiction. Harold Frederick's Theron Ware, Lewis's Elmer Gantry, and Faulkner's Whitfield are fairly typical. They are simple-minded, and readily satirized. Cary's God-driven men are grotesque vessels of grace, something like Flannery O'Connor's grotesque saint Hazel Motes, in *Wise Blood*. Everyone—the captives who accept orthodoxy, and the free, who go their own obsessed way—seeks salvation. Each seeks to justify his actions, and in doing so seeks realms that transcend self. Yet in seeking such realms they draw after them, or are pulled backward into, lusts, material aggrandizements of various sorts, and power. Cary would have it that despite this, the free, and sometimes the captives, discover a luminous reality, called beauty, love, or God.

This is Cary's doctrine. In certain of his novels the doctrine itself does not take fire—in *The Captive and the Free*, for example. The bush is there, but Cary, sick and facing his own death, could not make it burn.

In those last months before his death, Joyce Cary wanted desperately to finish *The Captive and the Free*. The title incidentally could serve as a statement of his persistent theme. He also worked hard to finish *Art and Reality*. The two sides of the man, the explainer and novelist, continued as though in tandem to the very end.

The questioners in the *Paris Review* interview saw in Cary's study many files and boxes of novels and short stories. Sometimes, he said, he interrupted his writing to block out an outline of 20,000 words of yet another story. For Cary life flowed turbulently, abundantly. Probably this is why his short stories, collected as *Spring Song* (1960), seem only outlines for novels. They are too terse to achieve either the comedy or vitality of the best novels. He needed a broad canvas, and perhaps this is why the two trilogies may prove to be his best work.

SELECTED BIBLIOGRAPHY

NOTE: *A considerable collection of Cary's unpublished manuscripts and papers is in the possession of the Bodleian Library.*

PRINCIPAL WORKS OF JOYCE CARY

Aissa Saved. London, Ernest Benn, 1932; London, Michael Joseph, 1949 (Carfax edition, 1952).
An American Visitor. London, Ernest Benn, 1933; London, Michael Joseph, 1952 (Carfax edition, 1952); New York, Harper, 1961.
The African Witch. London, Victor Gollancz, 1936; New York, William Morrow, 1936; London, Michael Joseph, 1950 (Carfax edition, 1951); New York, Harper, 1962.
Castle Corner. London, Victor Gollancz, 1938; London, Michael Joseph, 1950 (Carfax edition, 1952).
Mister Johnson. London, Victor Gollancz, 1939; London, Michael Joseph, 1947 (Carfax edition, 1952); New York, Harper, 1951; Harmondsworth, Penguin, 1964.
Power in Men. London, Nicholson and Watson, 1939. (Published for the Liberal Book Club.)
Charley Is My Darling. London, Michael Joseph, 1940 (Carfax edition, 1951); New York, Harper, 1960.
The Case for African Freedom. London, Secker and Warburg, 1941; revised and enlarged edition, 1944.
A House of Children. London, Michael Joseph, 1941 (Carfax edition, 1951); Harmondsworth, Penguin, 1955; New York, Harper, 1956.
Herself Surprised. London, Michael Joseph, 1941 (Carfax edition, 1951); Harmondsworth, Penguin, 1955; New York, Universal Library (Grosset and Dunlap), 1960. (Included, with To Be a Pilgrim and The Horse's Mouth, in First Trilogy. New York, Harper, 1958.)
To Be a Pilgrim. London, Michael Joseph, 1942 (Carfax edition, 1951); New York, Harper, 1949; Harmondsworth, Penguin, 1957; New York, Universal Library, 1960.
Process of Real Freedom. London, Michael Joseph, 1943.
The Horse's Mouth. London, Michael Joseph, 1944 (Carfax edition, 1951); Harmondsworth, Penguin, 1948; New York, Harper, 1950;

Andrew Wright, ed., London, George Rainbird, 1957; Andrew Wright, ed., New York, Harper's Modern Classics, 1959; New York, Universal Library, 1959.
Britain and West Africa. London, Longmans, Green, 1946; revised edition, 1947.
The Moonlight. London, Michael Joseph, 1946 (Carfax edition, 1952); New York, Harper, 1947.
A Fearful Joy. London, Michael Joseph, 1949 (Carfax edition, 1952); New York, Harper, 1950; Harmondsworth, Penguin, 1956; New York, Anchor Books (Doubleday), 1961.
"The Way a Novel Gets Written," *Harper's*, CC (February, 1950), 87–93; *Adam International Review*, XVIII (November–December, 1950), 3–11.
"The Novelist at Work: A Conversation between Joyce Cary and Lord David Cecil," *Adam International Review*, XVIII (November–December, 1950), 15–25.
Prisoner of Grace. London, Michael Joseph, 1952 (Carfax edition, 1954); New York, Harper, 1952.
Except the Lord. London, Michael Joseph, 1953; New York, Harper, 1953.
"An Interview with Joyce Cary," conducted by John Burrows and Alex Hamilton, *Paris Review*, VIII (Winter, 1954–55), 63–78. Reprinted in Malcolm Cowley, ed., Writers at Work: The Paris Review Interviews. New York, Viking, 1959, pp. 51–67.
Not Honour More. London, Michael Joseph, 1955; New York, Harper, 1955.
The Captive and the Free. London, Michael Joseph, 1959; New York, Harper, 1959; Harmondsworth, Penguin, 1964.
Spring Song and Other Stories. London, Michael Joseph, 1960; Harmondsworth, Penguin, 1964.
Memoir of the Bobotes (with illustrations by the author). London, Michael Joseph, 1964.

CRITICAL WORKS AND COMMENTARY

Adams, Hazard. "Blake and Gulley Jimson: English Symbolists," *Critique*, III (Spring–Fall, 1959), 3–14.
Allen, Walter. Joyce Cary. London, Longmans, Green, 1953; revised edition, 1954.
Bloom, Robert. The Indeterminate World. Philadelphia, University of Pennsylvania Press, 1961.

Hardy, Barbara. "Form in Joyce Cary's Novels," *Essays in Criticism*, IV (April, 1954), 180–90.
Harrison, Fairfax. The Devon Carys. 2 vols. New York, De Vinne Press, 1922.
Mahood, M. M. Joyce Cary's Africa. London, Methuen and Company, 1964.
Prescott, Orville. "Two Modern Masters: Cozzens, Cary," in In My Opinion. Indianapolis, Bobbs, Merrill, 1952, 180–99.
Ryan, Marjorie. "An Interpretation of Joyce Cary's *The Horse's Mouth*," *Critique*, II (Spring–Summer, 1958), 29–38.
Starkie Enid. "Joyce Cary, A Personal Portrait," *Virginia Quarterly Review*, XXXVII (Winter, 1961), 110–34.
Wright, Andrew. Joyce Cary: A Preface to His Novels. London; Chatto and Windus, 1958; New York, Harper, 1958.
——— "Joyce Cary's Unpublished Work," *London Magazine*, V (January, 1958), 35–42.
Young, William R. The Plantation in Ulster. London, Eyre, Spottiswoode, 1932.

GPSR Authorized Representative: Easy Access System Europe, Mustamäe tee 50, 10621 Tallinn, Estonia, gpsr.requests@easproject.com

www.ingramcontent.com/pod-product-compliance
Ingram Content Group UK Ltd.
Pitfield, Milton Keynes, MK11 3LW, UK
UKHW041654310326
469532UK00002B/18